AR 5.9
1 pT.

DRUGS AND DENIAL

Denying you have a drug problem is dangerous because it prevents you from getting the help you need.

THE DRUG ABUSE PREVENTION LIBRARY

DRUGS AND DENIAL

Wendy Klein

THE ROSEN PUBLISHING GROUP, INC.
NEW YORK

*For Jeff, who provided me with constant inspiration
and graciously volunteered to play many rounds of golf while I wrote;
and Erica, who kindly looked the other way when my deadlines slipped by.
Thanks and love to both!*

*The people pictured in this book are only models. They in no way practice or
endorse the activities illustrated. Captions serve only to explain the subjects of
photographs and do not in any way imply a connection between the real-life
models and the staged situations.*

Published in 1998 by The Rosen Publishing Group, Inc.
29 East 21st Street, New York, NY 10010

First Edition

Library of Congress Cataloging-in-Publication Data
Klein, Wendy.
    Drugs and denial / Wendy Klein.
    p.   cm. — (The drug abuse prevention library)
    Includes bibliographical references and index.
    ISBN 0-8239-2773-3
        1. Teenagers—drug use—Juvenile literature. 2. Drug
abuse—Juvenile literature. 3. Denial (Psychology)—Juvenile
literature.
        I. Title. II. Series.
        HV5824.Y68K57   1998
        362.29'12'0835—dc21   98-14709
                                                                     CIP

Manufactured in the United States of America

Contents

Introduction

Rosa was having a tough time adjusting to her new school. She kept to herself and spent most days going from home to school and back again without speaking a word to anyone. And since Rosa's mother worked a second job at night and her father didn't live with them, Rosa spent most evenings watching television. One day Rosa bumped into some girls drinking beer behind the school. When they offered her a drink, she didn't hesitate. "If I mess this up," Rosa thought as she tipped the bottle, "they'll never talk to me again."

It turned out that the girls did talk to Rosa again. They began drinking alcohol together every afternoon, and Rosa discovered that a couple of drinks really loosened her up and made it easier to joke around. "They like me," Rosa came to realize. "They think I'm as cool as they are!"

Eventually, the afternoon binges stretched |
into evenings. Rosa and her new friends moved
the parties to Rosa's house when the sun went
down. At first, Rosa loved hanging out with the
group and gossiping and goofing around. But
after a few months, Rosa really looked forward
to getting drunk.

Rosa didn't think about how much she
drank; she was making it to school every day,
and her grades were still good. She was proud
that she could drink more than anyone in her
crowd and not get hangovers. Then, in spring,
the whole school had to attend a special assem-
bly about drug abuse. Rosa sat in the back of
the auditorium giggling with her friends about
the speakers, who were all recovering alcoholics
and former drug users. When the principal
passed out a questionnaire for the students to
fill out about their drug-use habits, Rosa put
hers under the seat. She didn't need a stupid
piece of paper to tell her how to run her life.
Rosa ignored the stares from her friends as she
stood up and walked out of the room. She kept
going—out of the school, down the street, and
into her empty house. She flicked on the tele-
vision, kicked off her shoes, and then Rosa
grabbed a beer.

What You Will Learn from This Book

Using drugs, even using them just once,

8 can lead to serious trouble. People who use drugs often insist they can handle it. But it's important to realize that sooner or later drug use catches up to everybody. Drugs are dangerous substances and affect different people in different ways. Just because you can still make it to volleyball practice after a night of heavy partying doesn't mean you have everything under control.

It's much easier to ignore a problem with drugs than admit you might need help. And that's where this book comes in. It will let you know how to tell if someone is denying drug use—even if that someone is you.

We'll discuss some of the reasons why people use drugs as well as how to recognize the signs of addiction. Then you'll learn about denial and why ignoring a substance-abuse problem is risky. Next, you should understand the negative effects of enabling and codependency, and how even people with the best intentions can actually contribute to a drug problem. Finally, we'll address how to help someone in denial face up to his or her addiction—or, even better, learn how to prevent substance abuse before it starts.

Some of these issues may be painful to read about, especially if you're finally admitting a problem in yourself or someone you love. You have to keep telling yourself that denial is only the easy way out—not $\quad$ *9* the right way out. Ignoring a serious problem doesn't make the problem go away.

Facing up to drug addiction or con- fronting a friend in denial may be the hardest thing you ever do. But as you read this book, you'll discover some ways you can help someone admit to having a problem and get the treatment he or she needs. And you'll read more about other young people like Rosa. You'll see how they deal with their drug use and learn from their experiences.

Using drugs even once can lead to a serious problem.

CHAPTER 1

Why People Use Drugs

*C*arlos *looked up to his older brother, Juan. Juan was seventeen and did whatever he wanted to do whenever he wanted to do it. He always had a party going, and he never invited Carlos. Because Carlos admired his older brother so much, he felt hurt when Juan took off without him. Even though Carlos knew Juan and his friends drank and smoked pot at their parties, he still wanted to go with them.*

One night their mother told Juan she had to go out of town for a couple of days and he should look after Carlos. The moment she walked out of the door, Juan picked up the phone. Three hours later twenty kids were crammed into their two-bedroom apartment, and five more were coming through the door carrying a case of beer. "Carlos, get out of here.

12 | You're too young to be doin' this stuff," Juan warned. His eyes looked really red.

"Shut up, Juan. You better let me stay or I'll tell Mom what's going on!" Carlos knew there was nothing Juan could do. He smiled as he walked into his bedroom, swiping a drink off the counter on his way.

Later, finishing up his second drink, Carlos stumbled into the bathroom and found Juan with his friends in the hallway sucking on a balloon. They laughed when Carlos asked them what they were doing. "Hey, little man," one of the boys said, "wanna come do a whip-it with us?" Although Carlos didn't exactly know what a whip-it was, he knew he didn't want to do any drugs with his brother's friends. Liquor was one thing, he reasoned, drugs were something completely different.

But then Juan butted in, "Just leave him alone, guys. He's just a baby. He can't even handle a stupid bottle of beer—you think he could do this? Don't waste your goods on him!" Immediately, Carlos got defensive. He was sick of Juan's always telling him what to do. Just because Juan was older didn't make him all that smart! Carlos turned his back to his brother, and Juan stormed out of the room.

For a second, Carlos thought about following Juan, but then he saw how his brother's friends were looking at him. Laughing, they

showed him how to get high. Carlos was scared
*to do it, but he was more scared not to. He didn't
want to look like a jerk. So he carefully inhaled
the drug. Just when he thought nothing was
happening, the room went dark. And when he
finally opened his eyes, the room was still dark.*

*A couple days later—in the hospital—
Carlos discovered that his blindness might be
temporary, but the doctors weren't sure. They
explained that inhalants like whip-its can have
dramatic effects on users and no one can predict
the outcome. Carlos was going to have to wait
to find out if he would ever be able to see again.*

Drugs influence many aspects of our
lives. We swallow aspirin for a headache,
cough syrup for a cold. We drink caffeine
to wake up, and alcohol to calm down. But
how many of us think of these substances
as drugs? By definition, drugs change the
way our brain and body systems work.
They can be either legal, like aspirin, or
illegal, like amphetamines. And even legal
drugs prescribed by a doctor, like painkillers
after an operation, can be abused. You can
take too many, give some to your friends,
or use them in ways other than how they
were intended.

Take a minute to think how drugs affect
your life. Think about the advertising you

Although we may not think about it, most of us use drugs—even over-the-counter cough and cold medicine—at some time.

see in magazines or on television, or how your favorite actors smoke, drink, or take drugs in the movies. We see so many situations involving drugs, we rarely stop to think about the messages we're receiving. When we stop noticing things that were shocking or surprising the first time we saw them, it means we've become desensitized. And when you become desensitized to the idea of using drugs, it will get easier and easier to ignore and deny their dangerous effects.

So now that we realize we're surrounded by drugs, both legal and illegal, let's take a look at why people may want to try them.

Peer Pressure

You've probably heard how people try drugs because their friends encourage them to do it. Maybe you've been in a situation in which a friend of yours persuaded you to do something, like cheat on a math test, that you didn't really want to do—or knew was wrong to do. That's peer pressure. No matter how old you are, your friends' opinions are very important to you. That's why you have to choose the people you hang around with wisely. Of course, there's nothing wrong with wanting to be popular, but you should think seriously

Movies, television, and magazines often paint an unrealistic, glamorous picture of drug use.

about why the "popular" kids are so popular. Is it because they're good students and active in school activities? Or is it because they're wild party animals and can get any type of drug available? Which type of person would you rather be? What about five years from now?

Let's think back to Rosa, who began drinking when she started in a new school. She didn't like much about her friends except their popularity, and the girls mainly liked Rosa because they could drink at her house without getting caught. Rosa thought she was making friends, but she was only becoming addicted to alcohol. Think how different Rosa's life would have been if she hadn't felt that she had to impress the other girls by drinking.

Sometimes people can justify their actions when their friends go along with them. For instance, you may have heard people say they don't want to drink alone. Basically, they're really saying that they'll feel better about their own drinking if you indulge with them. They're using their position, as friends, to make you do something you don't want to do.

Rebellion

Most likely, you know that many drugs can

18 | cause harm. Your parents and teachers tell you over and over not to do drugs, that drugs will ruin your life. However, people often hear (and see in movies) that drugs can make them feel good and they want to test the results for themselves. They want to rebel against parents and teachers and act on their own—even if the outcome could cause harm to themselves or others.

Carlos mistakenly thought he could earn the respect of his brother's friends by taking drugs. When Carlos tried the whip-it, he rebelled against Juan's rules for drug use. Juan had specifically warned Carlos not to do any other drugs, but Carlos had ideas of his own. He resented being told how to act by his brother (and by anyone). Unfortunately, Carlos learned the truth about drug use the hard way.

CHAPTER 2

How to Spot a Problem

Jennifer borrowed her mom's car one night, picked up her best friend, Michele, and headed over to a nearby fraternity party. Even though the girls were only sixteen, they knew they'd have no trouble getting in the front door. Jennifer and Michele loved to dance, and since they considered themselves too mature for high school dances, they partied at university campuses. It was fun to go where no one knew them and they could act as crazy as they wanted to. Both girls looked forward to moving away and starting college in two years.

Everything was going great—Jennifer was dancing with a group of people, and Michele was busy flirting with a guy. It was only midnight, and they didn't have to be home until after one. When it was time to go, Jennifer started

20 | *looking around for Michele, who was nowhere to be seen. Just then, Michele came running to her and grabbed her arm. "Oh my God, Jenn, you gotta come back in here. Some guy'll let us try heroin for free! He says it's so much better than that 'X' we did last week. C'mon—they're all in the bathroom waiting for us."*

The two girls walked into the bathroom. Michele's new friend Dante handed them needles and showed them how to inject a tiny amount of heroin right into their veins. Jenn thought about the people she heard of who had overdosed on drugs. She remembered the night the Smashing Pumpkins had to cancel their concert because they found their drummer dead in the bathtub after he OD'd on heroin. And here they were, standing in a bathroom!

Meanwhile, Michele had already taken a hit and was slumped on the floor with a beautiful smile on her face. "Oh, Jenn," she said, "you gotta try this. It's just the most amazing feeling. You'll love it." So Jenn put out her arm and jammed the needle into her vein. Seconds later, she threw up all over herself, Dante, and Michele. She managed to grope her way out of the bathroom and out of the fraternity house. Despite the terrible itching she felt on her arms and face, Jenn walked five miles home.

When Jenn called Michele the next day, Michele said she was busy and couldn't do anything. Because Jenn was so embarrassed over what happened, she didn't call Michele again for a couple of weeks. But one day in school, Michele approached her. "Hey, Jenn, I know it's been awhile since we've talked and I want to apologize. Let's do something this weekend, okay? I'm sorry I haven't returned your calls." Jennifer was so happy to have her friend back, she gave Michele a big hug. "Sure, Michele. We can do whatever you want. I can get the car."

"Great!" Michele hugged her back. "Oh, Jenn—do you have any money on you? I need to get my mom a birthday present tonight and I'm kinda short. I'll pay you back later." Jennifer gave her $30, and they agreed to get in touch the next day.

Another week passed without Jenn hearing from Michele. She finally got so angry she went right over to Michele's house and rang the doorbell. "Hi Jenn," her mom said. "I thought Michele was staying at your house today and tonight. Why isn't she with you?" Taken by surprise, Jenn made up an excuse about meeting at the mall and took off. She thought she knew where to find her friend.

At the fraternity house, the guys said they hadn't seen Michele for a couple of days—and they were glad they hadn't. She was getting to be a big problem, always sniffing around for

Friends who are addicted to a drug may ask you to loan them money for one reason and instead spend it on drugs.

more heroin, and never having any money to pay for it. In fact, when Jenn found her, would she please tell Michele to stay away? They were sick of dealing with her!

Jenn finally caught up with Michele that night outside of another fraternity house. Michele was begging some guy at the door to sell her heroin. She didn't believe it when he said he didn't have any. Michele just thought he wanted more money for it. As Jenn walked up to her friend, she heard Michele say, "Look, I don't have any more money on me now. But I can pay you in other ways, you know. Can't we work something out?"

When we say that someone is addicted to drugs, we mean that he or she depends on a chemical and will do almost anything to get it. Essentially, the drug becomes the most important thing in his or her life. That's what happened to Michele. She was so desperate to get heroin, she was willing to do anything—even prostitute herself—to get some.

Addiction usually takes two forms: physical and psychological. When you're physically addicted to a drug, you develop a tolerance to its effects (you find that you need more and more of the drug in order to get the same high). You will also suffer withdrawal symptoms when you stop taking the drug. When you're psychologically addicted, you think you need to take a drug even though there may be no physical reason to do so. Psychological addiction still gives you very real symptoms, like hallucinations. People who hallucinate may see things that aren't really there, like bugs crawling on their bodies.

The younger you are, the quicker you will become physically and psychologically addicted to drugs. Scientists are not exactly sure why this is so; basically, they think it's because the brains and bodies of teens are still developing and are at a higher risk of nerve and brain-cell damage. Also, because we are all unique individuals and each drug

Hallucinations can result from drug use.

is different, there's no guarantee how much | **25**
damage drug abuse can do. Remember, the
manufacture of illegal drugs is not regu-
lated by the government, so we don't know
what they contain. For example, although
Jennifer and Michele took hits from the
same batch of heroin, we can see how dif-
ferently they reacted.

The Signs of Addiction

No one is immune to drug addiction,
whether it's physical or psychological. Let's
take a look at some of the signs of addiction. If you or someone you know can
answer yes to any part of four or more of
these questions, you may be dealing with a
drug problem.

1. Do you think about drugs constantly
   when you're not taking them? Maybe
   you used to think about school,
   sports, or your friends, but now you
   even dream about taking drugs.
2. Do you increase the amounts you
   take? Did you start out drinking one
   beer and now you can drink three or
   four?
3. Do you need to take larger doses to
   get high? Do you think the drug's
   effects wear off more quickly than
   they used to?

4. Do you feel withdrawal symptoms when you're not using? Do your hands shake when you wake up? Do you have headaches?

5. Do you use drugs to control withdrawal symptoms? If your hands shake in the morning, do you drink to make the shaking stop?

6. Have you made repeated efforts to cut back or stop using drugs? Do you stop using for a couple of days, or take smaller doses, only to continue using the following week?

7. Is it hard for you to continue your everyday activities because of drug use? Did you quit an after-school club or sport because it interfered with parties? Is it difficult to wake up for school because you were up late the night before taking drugs?

8. Would you rather use drugs alone than with your friends? Are you concerned you won't get "enough" drugs because you have to share with friends? When you take drugs with your friends, do they tell you you've had enough or should stop? Do you take drugs alone so they won't hassle you?

9. Do you continue to take drugs after having drug-related social, emotional,

Drug users may hang out with friends who use drugs or cut school in order to take drugs.

and physical problems? Have you been feeling unusually depressed, angry, moody, or violent? Have your closest friends stopped hanging out with you? Does your nose bleed? Do you feel extremely nervous and anxious? Does your attention span seem shorter?

The Four Stages of Adolescent Drug Use

Doctors and other professionals believe adolescents (generally, people between the ages of twelve and eighteen) may go through slightly different stages of drug addiction than adults do. When adolescents use drugs, they tend to party and hang out with people they know will have drugs with

28 | them. In addition to other substances they take, kids using hard drugs often drink hard liquor and smoke pot. They're frequently drunk or high at school. If you suspect your friends use drugs, try to see if they follow any of these patterns:

1. First, teens using drugs will experiment with substances until they learn what to expect from each. As they "learn the mood swing," they become more accustomed to how drugs will affect them.

2. Next, drug users "seek the mood swing." They may hang out only with friends who use drugs, and they may cut school in order to take drugs.

3. By now, it's common for users to think about drugs constantly and take them on a daily basis. They become "obsessed with the mood swing."

4. Finally, teens take drugs not for the mood swing but to feel "normal." At this point, they're probably also experiencing physical withdrawal symptoms when they're not using drugs.

CHAPTER 3

Why Denial Is Dangerous

*D*irk figured high school would be a breeze. He always got straight A's in middle school and expected to do the same now. Even though it was summer, every day Dirk went to the library to study. He knew he had to do exceptionally well to get into a good college. He knew it because his parents seemed to tell him that every hour or so. He tried to concentrate on his reading list, but the weather was beautiful and he wanted to play basketball with his friends.

On the first night before school, Dirk slept like a baby. He couldn't wait to start his new classes and meet new people. But as he went to each class and wrote down his homework assignments, Dirk started to get scared. He already had three quizzes scheduled on the same day next week, and he couldn't find his

30 | *friends during lunch. Dirk planned to start his homework the second he got home.*

"I can do this," Dirk thought. "As long as I study every night for three hours, I'll be able to keep up with everything." And he did try to keep the grueling routine he set for himself. But school got even more difficult for Dirk once his after-school activities started—and then he began hanging out on weekends with a girl named Caitlin.

When he brought home his first report card, Dirk's parents were less than thrilled with his C in Algebra. "What happened, Dirk?" his father demanded. "I thought you said everything was fine. You're not going to get into a good college with grades like these. Forget about that homecoming party this Saturday. Forget about your girlfriend Caitlin! You're studying."

Caitlin was angry that Dirk had so little time to spend with her, and she threatened to break up with him. She didn't see why he had to study all the time anyway; she got average grades and no one hassled her. Out of desperation, Dirk agreed to meet Caitlin when his parents went to bed.

So that night after his dad checked his homework, Dirk pretended to go to bed early. Soon after he heard his mom and dad turn in, Dirk left the house to find Caitlin. And when Dirk tiptoed back to his bedroom at three in the morning, he thought things were back on track.

Even though some drugs can be purchased over the counter,
they still can be harmful if not taken correctly.

32 It was a hard schedule to maintain and Dirk started falling asleep in school. Then, because he was sleeping through so many classes, he had to work extra hard at home. But the last straw came when Dirk fell asleep and missed a couple of dates with Caitlin. So he bought some caffeine capsules at the drug store that promised to keep him awake. Since the label on the package said the pills were "no stronger than two cups of coffee," Dirk figured it would be okay to take them.

At first the pills really seemed to help. Dirk felt so energetic—he rushed home from school, rushed through his homework, and was awake for his all-night dates with Caitlin. Even Dirk's parents were pleased when he got an A on his next Algebra test. Dirk felt on top of the world. "I can do this," he told himself. Meanwhile, he was going through half a bottle of pills a day.

It wasn't long before Dirk couldn't fall asleep at all. His eyes were always bloodshot, and he was too nervous to eat. He avoided mealtimes at home, telling his parents, "I have to go study now—big test coming up, you know." But whenever he opened a book, he fidgeted so much he couldn't get any reading done.

Caitlin hated how Dirk never listened to her anymore. She thought he was making fun of her when he paced back and forth or tapped *his foot when she tried to talk to him. Dirk felt bad about hurting his girlfriend, but his body seemed to have a mind of its own. The worst part was lying in bed for hours, his mind racing, and thinking about how tired he was going to be the next day if he didn't get some sleep.*

One night Dirk just knew he wasn't going to fall asleep. His stomach was jumping around and he couldn't relax, no matter how many sheep he counted. He walked into the bathroom to brush his teeth for the third time that night. As he put the toothpaste back into the cabinet, Dirk noticed the pain pills that the doctor pre-scribed for his mom after dental surgery. The label of the bottle read, "May cause drowsi-ness." Dirk opened the bottle and looked inside. It was full. His mother would never notice if he took one or two, Dirk reasoned, as he popped some in his mouth. It worked like a charm.

Dirk took the caffeine pills in the morning and throughout the day to stay awake and study. Before bed he took a couple of his mom's pills to fall asleep. He could see nothing wrong with his new habits. "These pills aren't real drugs. A doctor said it's okay to take the painkillers, and the others you can buy in any pharmacy without a prescription. The store wouldn't sell them if they were dangerous." Dirk thought he had it all figured out.

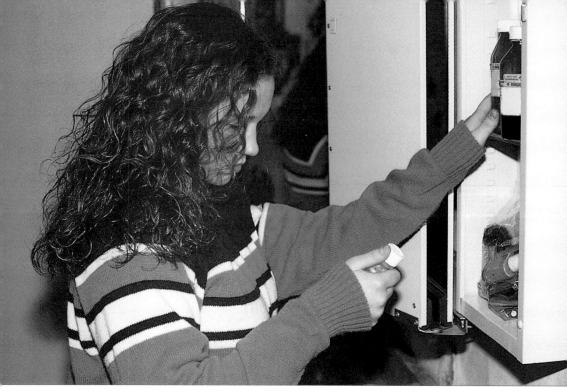

Taking medication not prescribed for you can be dangerous.

"Anyway, I have to do something. Mom and Dad are really leaning on me to get better grades. It's hard."

But Dirk failed to take into account that he didn't need the pills anymore. Since Caitlin had broken up with him a month ago, he didn't have to stay awake all night. He also seemed to "forget" that his grades were dropping steadily.

Dirk couldn't forget, however, that his mom's pills were almost gone, and he didn't know what he would do then. He thought it was time he stopped taking them, anyway. Maybe.

Admitting you have a problem—especially a problem with drugs—is a very hard thing to do. On the other hand, denying a problem with drugs is very easy to do. Denial acts as a blindfold to reality. As long as you deny your addiction, you'll never be able to see how harmful drugs are. Until you actually come forward and say "I am addicted to drugs," there isn't much hope for recovery. Let's look at the three components of denial and see how they progress from one to another:

The Three Components of Denial

1. Rationalization. When people attempt to explain or justify their drug use, they are rationalizing. They are trying to come up with (what they think are) logical reasons for taking drugs. Dirk thought he would lose Caitlin if he couldn't stay up to meet her during the night. However, these reasons are usually believable only to the user.

2. Projection. Sometimes people blame their drug use on other people. Remember how Dirk said he never would have used drugs if his parents hadn't expected him to do well in school? He was projecting his addiction onto his mom and dad.

3. Minimization. Even if drug users do admit to a habit, they may pretend

36 to use drugs much less than they really do. By minimizing the seriousness of drugs they're using, they can pretend they don't have a problem at all. Dirk tried to minimize his drug use by telling himself that the caffeine pills and painkillers weren't really strong or dangerous.

Why Denial Hurts You

Denying that you have a drug problem is dangerous because it prevents you from getting the help you need.

The longer you go on taking drugs, the greater chance you have of becoming addicted. And by the time you realize using drugs is no longer "fun," but something you *have* to do, you're already addicted. Drug addiction—and denial—can sneak up on you. And denial makes the beginning stages of addiction really easy to explain away.

Dirk truly thought he didn't have a problem with drugs because a medical doctor prescribed them. He didn't consider that the pills were for his mom, not for him. Dirk was also convinced that he could quit if he wanted to. We often hear the popular phrase, "I can quit anytime." These words often run through the mind of people addicted to drugs. They like to believe they are in control of their habits, whether or not they really are.

CHAPTER 4

Enabling and Codependency

DJ Williams was flying high. He had just graduated from high school, traveled to Europe, and was now ready to begin his first full-time job as an assistant manager in a popular coffee shop. He couldn't wait to start saving money so he could move out of his mother's house into a studio apartment downtown. Life was good. And things at home were good, too. Since he graduated, his family had been treating him like an adult. He no longer had a curfew or had to be home for dinner.

DJ took his job seriously. He never called in sick or showed up late, as he used to when he worked at a grocery store. And the manager and store owner took notice of DJ and encouraged him. "Hey, DJ," the manager told him, "this store could use more people like you. If you work really hard, who knows? Maybe you could open up your own place someday." His own place! DJ liked the sound of that. He decided that running his own coffee shop was a goal worth working for.

One of the best things about the job were the people. DJ was an easygoing guy who made friends quickly. So when his coworker Vinnie invited him to a party over the weekend, DJ couldn't wait to go—especially when Vinnie told him Tasha would be there, too. Tasha worked with DJ, and DJ had a big crush on her.

By the time DJ arrived at the party, everyone was wasted. Vinnie met him at the door with a big goofy grin. "Where were you, dude? Tasha was asking for you." DJ's stomach gave a little jump. He wasn't going to waste this opportunity. DJ walked confidently into the room where Vinnie was pointing. And there was Tasha, surrounded by a group of friends, laughing. She had a bottle of beer in one hand and a cigarette in the other. DJ waved in her direction, trying to catch her attention. He walked a little closer. But at that moment, just before she saw him, Tasha bent her head over a hand-held mirror and snorted some white powder into her nose.

"Hi, baby! We didn't think you were goin' to make it. You look great!" Tasha gave him a

Addicts see drugs as a way to have fun, not for the dangerous substances they really are.

kiss hello. "C'mon back here. Want some blow?
My treat, working boy." Without a second
thought, DJ allowed Tasha to grab his hand
and lead him to the mirror. He watched as she
spilled some cocaine from a vial onto the shiny
surface, chopped it up with a razor blade, and
offered it to him. DJ made a big show of inhal-
ing the coke and everyone laughed as he licked
up the last traces to make sure none of it went
to waste. "Man, that's some top grade stuff you
got there," DJ said. "Who do I have to thank
for it?"

Tasha stepped up, "That's from my own per-
sonal stash. I get it from my brother, so I know
it's pure. And you can thank me by dancing
with me. I just love this song." And from that
moment on, DJ and Tasha knew they belonged
together.

With Tasha for a girlfriend, DJ felt he could
do anything. They worked side by side at the
coffee shop until Tasha had to leave for class.
Then she'd come back to the store and study
while DJ closed up. After work, they were free
to do practically anything, and they never had
to look far for something fun to do. There was
always a party going on, and Tasha always
had some cocaine to contribute. At first she was
generous with her drugs and graciously offered
some to everyone. But then DJ complained
that she was giving it all away to people they

42 | *didn't even know. Why not just throw her money down the toilet, he said.*

After that, Tasha and DJ kept the cocaine to themselves. They thought the rush they got from the coke made life exciting. But one day Tasha's brother said he was cutting off her supply.

"What! What does he mean 'cutting you off?'" DJ asked. "He's crazy, Tasha. We're not drug addicts or nothing. It's just a social thing for us. Didn't you tell him that, Tasha? Didn't you?"

"Look," Tasha told DJ, "there's nothing I can do about it. Once my brother makes up his mind, that's it. We'll just have to find another source. I'll work more hours. Or we'll cut back on the blow. We said we were gonna quit anyway. It'll be okay."

Once again, their friend Vinnie came through for them. He knew some guy who could sell them more cocaine. It wouldn't be cheap, but Vinnie could guarantee the quality. DJ and Tasha jumped at the opportunity. And the first time they tried the new dealer, they were well satisfied. Everything seemed all right. "Let the party begin!" DJ exclaimed.

At home, Tasha's brother figured since he wasn't giving any more coke to Tasha, she must have quit. He ignored the fact that she rarely hung out with the family or that sometimes her

eyes were bloodshot and she was really jumpy.
*And the one time when her brother asked her
why her nose was all red and runny, Tasha just
said she had a cold. After that, he let her go her
own way. Tasha could tell he worried about her;
sometimes she thought he even seemed a little
scared of her. She tried not to think about it.*

*When Tasha told DJ that her brother thought
she was a drug addict, DJ was quick to reassure
her. "Look, Tasha, your brother doesn't know
what he's talking about. He just doesn't want
you cutting into his customer base. He probably
thought you were buying the coke cheap from
him and reselling it at work for top dollar. He's
insane, baby." And with that, they made plans
to meet their dealer that night.*

Enabling

Sometimes the people who love us the
most can be our biggest stumbling block in
overcoming a drug problem. For instance,
friends and relatives offer misguided help
when they make excuses for drug use. They
just don't want to admit that you have a
problem—and they make it easy for you to
join in their denial. People like this are
called enablers because they enable you to
continue using drugs.

You saw a classic enabler in Tasha's
brother. Not only did he provide her with

Some people would rather believe the lies of a drug abuser than admit there is a problem.

cocaine at first, but he wanted so badly to
think his little sister wasn't addicted to
drugs, he was willing to risk her health
rather than deal with a problem. Under-
standably, you don't want to think people
you love could be in trouble, and you really
want to believe that they're okay. And since
DJ was using the same amount of drugs as
Tasha, he wasn't about to accuse her of
having a problem. If he did that, he would
be admitting that he had the same
problem. So when Tasha complained that
her brother was worried about her, DJ tried
to convince Tasha that she was absolutely
fine.

Codependency

Any two people in a relationship
(mother/daughter, boyfriend/girlfriend,
friend/friend) depend on each other. When
two people like DJ and Tasha are in a dysfunctional relationship—one that doesn't
work normally—they can become dependent on each other's bad habits. Then,
when one person changes and ends the
habit, the whole nature of the relationship
shifts. When the habit is no longer there,
the people don't know why they're
together. In fact, without the habit to keep
it going, the relationship may dissolve.

46 People who are in a codependent relationship go through several stages:

1. They don't mind inappropriate
   behavior.
2. They lose the ability to be honest
   and admit to their problems.
3. They suffer severe mood swings,
   from feeling resigned to their problems to feeling responsible and ready
   to change them.
4. They withdraw from their families
   and friends.
5. They move toward intolerance, alter-
   nating between rage and panic.
6. They become isolated, discouraged,
   and fearful.

Anyone who's involved in a codependent relationship should find professional
help—with either a counselor or psycholo-
gist. You'll read more about how to do that
later in the book.

CHAPTER 5

Prevention and Intervention

*W*eek after week Nancy watched as her daughter Morgan changed from an outgoing high school junior with lots of friends to a sullen, withdrawn girl who spent all her spare time locked in her bedroom. At first, Nancy assumed Morgan was going through a phase— or maybe fighting with her boyfriend. But when she received a call from the school that Morgan hadn't shown up for her classes all week, Nancy knew something was going on.

"Morgan, honey, just tell me what's wrong. You never see your friends anymore, you never eat—you even quit the soccer team. I'm really worried about you. We used to be able to talk about anything, and now I feel as if I don't even know you." Nancy began to cry as Morgan rolled over on the bed and faced the

48 *wall. "Look, Mom, I don't want to talk about it. Nothing's wrong. I'm absolutely fine. Honest." Finally, Nancy gave up and left the room.*

Nancy came home from work one day to find Morgan's best friend Tracy sitting on the doorstep. "Hi, Tracy, long time no see!" Nancy had always liked Tracy; she seemed like such a good kid and a positive influence on Morgan.

"Mrs. Eagan, I need to tell you something. It's about Morgan. I found pot in her gym locker. I think she's taking drugs. And probably more than pot. I've thought about it for a long time and I didn't know what to do. Morgan hasn't show up for school all week and she's been ignoring me for months. I just didn't know what to do..."

Tracy paused as Nancy answered the ringing phone. It was Morgan. She said she was spending the night at Tracy's house and would be home the next day after school. Nancy hung up without another word. She didn't want to frighten Morgan away.

The next afternoon Nancy and Tracy went downtown to see a drug counselor. James talked to them about drug addiction, and how young people can become dependent on drugs very quickly. He also warned them that Morgan might not be ready to admit to a problem.

If you know that a friend has a drug problem, talk to his or her parents or another adult you trust.

"It's hard to help people who don't want to be helped," James told Nancy and Tracy. "I know. I used to be addicted to crack." He suggested that they set up an intervention and invite Morgan's closest drug-free friends and family members.

The next day Nancy, Tracy, James, and Morgan's ex-boyfriend Sean sat in the Eagans' living room waiting for Morgan to arrive. James reviewed with the others what to say and how to act. "Morgan's going to think we're ganging up on her," Tracy worried.

"The point is to keep talking calmly to Morgan until she realizes that we're here to help her. That we're here because we care. I'm going to keep things under control. I'll make sure she gets herself into a good rehab program—one that'll really help her," James

50 said. *"It's important that only one person talk at a time and bring up specific examples of Morgan's drug use and how she lies about using. We need to show her that we're not making anything up, that this is for real."*

When Morgan finally came home, she looked shocked to see everyone waiting for her. "What the hell is going on here?" she demanded. Nancy put her arms around her daughter. "Morgan, we want to help you. This man here is a drug counselor. He helps people who are addicted to drugs, honey. It's okay, Morgan—we know. We all know you've been taking drugs."

One by one, they all stood up and gave evidence of Morgan's drug addiction. Sean said he broke up with her because he couldn't stand to watch what she was doing to herself. Tracy revealed how hurt she had been when Morgan stopped talking to her after Tracy wouldn't use drugs one night. Eventually they talked themselves out. They stood silently as Morgan's expressions changed from shock, to anger, to fear. She didn't respond to their comments, not even to deny them. Morgan just looked extremely tired. And when James asked if she wanted his help to come clean, she nodded her head without a word.

Even though drug addiction is extremely serious, it is possible to recover. It takes a

Speaking with a trained professional can help you overcome a drug or alcohol problem.

lot of hard work from you as well as a lot of help from your friends and family. Once you make up your mind to break free of your addiction, and realize you can't do it alone, you need to consider the next step—your treatment options.

How to Help People Who Want Help
If a friend of yours is seeking help for a drug problem, the first thing you should do is find someone responsible who can contact a drug counselor or a doctor. The most important thing is to find an expert who can recommend the right program. Inpatient treatment is given in special facilities where people live from several weeks up to several months. There, patients can

52 | depend on a staff trained to deal with both physical and psychological withdrawal difficulties. Everyone has to attend group meetings led by psychologists and therapists to discuss the effects drugs have had on their lives.

Some people choose to join outpatient treatment programs in which they can work on their problems at home with their families and friends. They may also attend group meetings held in their community, like Alcoholics Anonymous or Narcotics Anonymous. People who choose this type of option tend to have a supportive relationship with their families. The lines of communication have to stay open and honest, which may be difficult for teens with dysfunctional or codependent families.

Getting Through to People Who Don't Want Help

People who take drugs don't always want to stop. Most likely, they deny they have any problem at all. People in this type of situation are not easy to confront. But if you know the warning signs that someone is using drugs, you may be able to help. If your friend brushes you off and tells you not to worry, that might be cause for concern.

Confronting someone about her drug use is never easy.

Teens in denial will tell you nothing's wrong, that they're still functioning, still making it to school every day. They may tell you they can stop using drugs at any time. They may even stop using for a couple of days, to show you that they're not addicted. But remember that you don't have to use drugs every second of every day to be addicted.

Sometimes it takes drastic measures to help teens stop using drugs. An intervention is a carefully planned meeting during which friends and family confront someone about his or her drug use. It's usually a last attempt to shock users into admitting they're struggling with a substance-abuse problem. As we saw with Morgan, the

54 | intervention included everyone who had evidence of her drug use. It could be teachers, friends, or relatives, as long as they're close to the teen and have some positive influence over his or her actions. The idea of an intervention is to provide so many examples of abusive behavior that the teen can't deny his or her drug use any longer. Because an intervention can be such an overwhelming experience, it is important to have a trained professional to guide the situation and suggest appropriate follow-up procedures. If you're thinking of an intervention, be sure to contact someone who has expert experience.

It *is* possible to confront and change denial when you have the right support.

Glossary

codependency Relationship in which one person abuses drugs and the other makes the abuse possible.

defensive Behavior intended to protect one from attack.

desensitized Become accustomed to a possibly dangerous condition or situation.

dysfunctional No longer operating in a normal or useful way.

enabling Making possible; in drug abuse, helping a user continue to continue his or her addiction.

hallucination Seeing or hearing things that are not there.

inhalants Common substances that produce a high when inhaled.

intervention Method of trying to reach a substance abuser by showing him or her all the pain being inflicted on loved ones.

56 | **intolerance** Failure to give social, political, or religious rights to others.
justifying Showing or trying to show that one's behavior is correct or reasonable.
whip-it A type of inhalant.

Where to Go for Help

Yellow Pages of Telephone Book
Drug Abuse, Counseling, Social Services
  Organizations

White Pages of Telephone Book
Community Services, Drug Abuse Hotline

**School Counselors, School Nurse,
  Drug Education and Student Services**

Toughlove
PO Box 1069
Doylestown, PA 18901

**Center on Addiction and Substance
  Abuse**
Columbia University
152 West 57th Street
New York, NY 10019
(212) 841-5200

58 | **Narcotics Anonymous**
World Service Office, USA
PO Box 9999
Van Nuys, CA 91409
(818) 773-9999
e-mail: wso@aol.com

National Institute on Alcohol Abuse
  and Alcoholism
PO Box 2345
Rockville, MD 20852
(800) 729-6686

Al-Anon Family Group Headquarters
1600 Corporate landing Parkway
Virginia Beach, VA 23456
(804) 563-1600
(800) 344-2666
Web site: http://www.al-anon.org/

In Canada
Alcohol and Drug Dependency Infor-
  mation and Counseling Services
  (ADDICS)
#2, 2471 1/2 Portage Avenue
Winnipeg, MB R3J 0N6
Canada

Alcoholics Anonymous, Toronto
#502 Intergroup Office
234 Eglinton Avenue E
Toronto, ON M4P 1K5
Canada

Narcotics Anonymous, Ontario
World Service Office
150 Britannia Road East, Unit 21
Mississauga, ON L4Z 2A4
Canada
(416) 507-0100

For Further Reading

Clayton, Dr. Lawrence. *Designer Drugs*, rev. ed. New York: Rosen Publishing Group, 1997.

Daley, Dennis. *Adolescent Relapse Prevention Workbook*. New York: Learning Publications, 1991.

——. *Focus on Addictions*. Santa Barbara: ABC-Clio, 1992.

Forrest, Gary G. *How to Cope with a Teenage Drinker*. South Orange, NJ: Jason Aronson, 1997.

Hicks, John. *Drug Addiction*. Brookfield, CT: Millbrook Press, 1997.

McMillan, Daniel. *Winning the Battle Against Drugs*. Danbury, CT: Franklin Watts, 1991.

Oliver, Marilyn Tower. *Drugs*. Springfield, NJ: Enslow Publishers, 1996.

Peck, Rodney G. *Crack*, rev. ed. New York: Rosen Publishing Group, 1997.

Porterfield, Kay Marie. *Coping with Code-pendency*, rev. ed. New York: Rosen Publishing Group, 1997.

Stamper, Laura. *When the Drug War Hits Home*. Minneapolis: Fairview Press, 1997.

Index

64 | ***About The Author***
Wendy Klein is a graduate of Indiana University of Pennsylvania, with a BA degree in English. She is currently employed at a large publishing company in New York City and lives in New Jersey.

Photo Credits
Cover photo by Les Mills; pgs. 16, 22, 27, 40 by Ira Fox; p. 24 by Olga Vega; p.51 by Seth Dinnerman; all other photos by John Novajosky